A Trip to Capitol Hill

by Sharon Franklin

Scott Foresman
is an imprint of

Glenview, Illinois • Boston, Massachusetts • Chandler, Arizona
Upper Saddle River, New Jersey

ISBN 13: 978-0-328-51795-4
ISBN 10:   0-328-51795-X

4 5 6 7 8 9 10 V0FL 15 14 13 12 11

Talk about living history! My aunt took me on a trip to Washington, D.C. Before we left, she asked me what I wanted to see most, and I knew my answer at once. I wanted to see the U.S. Capitol. Imagine seeing something in person that you have only read about in books. My teacher asked me to present a report to the class about my trip.

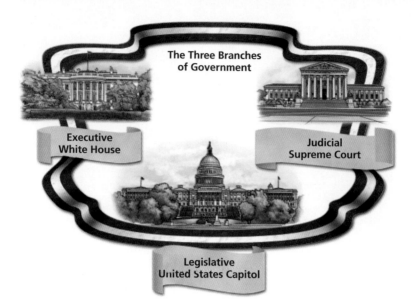

The Three Branches
of Government

Executive
White House

Judicial
Supreme Court

Legislative
United States Capitol

Before we left, I did some research. Here are some notes I made for my report.

The Founding Fathers tried to make sure that no one person had too much power. They also knew that a growing nation needed a strong government. They wrote the **Constitution** to deal with these challenges. In it, they outlined three branches, or parts, of government: legislative, executive, and judicial.

Each branch has **responsibility** for different jobs. Together, the three branches are designed to make sure the government runs smoothly and protects the rights of its citizens. Each branch has the power to challenge the other two branches. This system of checks and balances prevents any one branch from having too much power.

Legislative Branch

The legislative branch, or Congress, includes the House of Representatives and the Senate. This branch makes the country's laws. Citizens of each state vote for their own members of the House and Senate.

The number of members in the House is based on population. So states with more people have more representatives. But all states elect two senators each.

Among the powers of Congress are
- writing, discussing, and passing bills;
- declaring war on another country;
- making laws that control trade; and
- making laws regarding taxes and money.

Executive Branch

The executive branch makes sure that laws are obeyed and government policies are carried out. It is made up of the President, the Vice President, the Cabinet, and agency and department heads.

The President **solemnly** swears to uphold the Constitution. The President

- is commander-in-chief of the armed forces;
- chooses Cabinet members and oversees federal agencies;
- can veto bills passed by Congress; and
- can nominate federal judges.

To run for President, you must be a natural-born citizen, be at least 35 years old, and have lived in the United States for at least 14 years. The President is elected for a four-year term and may be re-elected for one more four-year term.

Judicial Branch

The Supreme Court is the highest court in the United States. It is made up of judges called justices. The President nominates all Supreme Court justices, including the Chief Justice of the United States. The Senate then must approve the President's choice.

The courts decide what laws mean, how they are applied, and whether they uphold the Constitution. This is how the judicial branch checks and balances decisions made by the legislative and executive branches.

The U.S. Capitol Building

We arrived in Washington, D.C., and found that the many buildings tell the story of our nation's history. The Capitol building was built from 1793 to 1826 as the first meeting place of Congress.

First I noticed the big round dome. The original building included the dome, and the Senate and House wings. As the United States grew, more legislators were needed to deal with the nation's **politics.** The Capitol became too small. In 1857 and 1859, new Senate and House chambers were added.

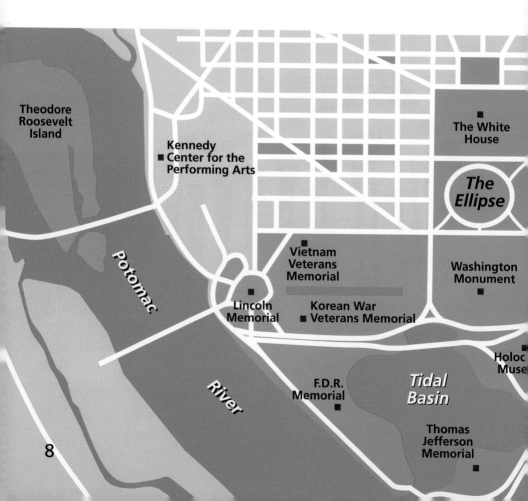

The Tour Begins

Many important buildings stand along the National Mall:

The Capitol
White House
Washington Monument
Lincoln Memorial
Jefferson Memorial
Vietnam Memorial
and other memorials

This Mall stretches two miles from the Capitol to the Lincoln Memorial. Many great museums surround the Mall:

Smithsonian Institution
National Gallery of Art
National Air and Space Museum
National Archives

My aunt and I arrived in Washington, D.C., and headed for Capitol Hill.

Union Station

National Archives

National Gallery of Art

seum
nerican
story

Museum of Natural History

The Supreme Court

M a l l

h e

United States Capitol

Smithsonian Institution

Air & Space Museum

The Library of Congress

Capitol Rotunda

The Rotunda is the round room beneath the dome. The round painting at the top of the dome, completed in 1865, includes 13 figures that represent the original 13 colonies. A bronze statue called *Armed Freedom* stands outside on top of the dome.

The newest work of art was added in 1997. It is a sculpture honoring three women who promoted the right of women to vote. They were Lucretia Mott, Elizabeth Cady Stanton, and Susan B. Anthony.

Library of Congress

If you like to read books, this is the place to visit. Imagine a library with about 532 miles of bookshelves; more than 29 million books; and almost 95 million maps, drawings, photographs, recordings, and other materials! There is such a library. It is the Library of Congress.

The Library is a resource for Congress and the American people. People use the Library of Congress to find documents from history.

House Office Buildings

In the original Capitol building, the House of Representatives had one wing. Today, there are four buildings: the Cannon, Longworth, Rayburn, and Ford House Office Buildings.

The House buildings have offices and meeting space for the many House committees. The Rayburn building has a bronze statue of former Speaker of the House Sam Rayburn. This building even has a subway to the Capitol! That must be very nice, especially on days when it is snowing and the wind is **howling.**

Senate Office Buildings

The Senate has three office buildings for the senators and staff: the Russell, Dirksen, and Hart Senate Office buildings. *Mountains and Clouds*, a 70-foot sculpture, is displayed in the Hart Senate Office Building.

Inside the Senate and House office buildings, senators and representatives write and enact laws for the country. Senators are elected to six-year terms, representatives to two-year terms.

Mountains and Clouds by Alexander Calder

Botanic Garden Conservatory

The Botanic Garden is the last stop on our tour. It is not only restful and beautiful, but it is also the oldest botanic garden in North America. It has an amazing variety of plants that botanists, or plant scientists, can use for studying and learning.

The botanists who work at the garden keep track of special historical plants and gifts from other countries. They list rare plants and collect medicinal plants that can't be found elsewhere.

Looking Ahead

For more than 200 years, the U.S. Capitol has preserved many reminders of our nation's **humble** beginnings, in the walls, grounds, and art of the buildings and open spaces. Our tour made me feel proud that I am a part of our country's history.

I also learned about all the people it takes to run a country. It would be interesting to work in the Capitol. I may sound **vain,** but seeing the Capitol buildings made me want to become a great leader myself someday. But for now, I will finish this report so I can present it to the class tomorrow.

Glossary

Constitution *n.* document that establishes the basic principles of the U.S. government.

howling *adj.* crying, wailing, shrieking.

humble *adj.* meek, modest.

politics *n.* the art or science of governing or of policies.

responsibility *n.* job, duty, task.

solemnly *adv.* seriously, earnestly

vain *adj.* proud, inflated.